THE EXPANSE OF ALL THINGS

poems

THE EXPANSE OF ALL THINGS

poems

JAMES SCOTT SMITH

Homebound Publications
Ensuring that the mainstream isn't the only stream.

Published in 2018 by Homebound Publications
Front Cover Image © James Scott Smith
Cover and Interior Designed by Leslie M. Browning
ISBN 978-1-947003-60-6
First Edition Trade Paperback

Homebound Publications
Ensuring the mainstream isn't the only stream.
WWW.HOMEBOUNDPUBLICATIONS.COM

10 9 8 7 6 5 4 3 2 1

Homebound Publications is committed to ecological stewardship. We greatly value the natural environment and invests in environmental conservation. Our books are printed on paper with chain of custody certification from the Forest Stewardship Council, Sustainable Forestry Initiative, and the Program for the Endorsement of Forest Certification.

ALSO BY THE AUTHOR

Water, Rocks and Trees

Contents

III

"My heart must open to the cosmos with no language unless we invent it moment by moment in order to breathe."

–JIM HARRISON

I

Mystic

If you are one
the wild God
wants for his own.
If you are drawn
into the silence, near
the bottom, along the edges.
If you have borne up under
some great catechism
and now are released of it,
into the world,
sure of not knowing
yet knowing for sure that
many acquisitions
had once worked
to convince you of many things,
contrived and contorted, to
which you never fully gave
your heart,
you
just might be
the mystic
you once dreamed of meeting
along the way.
And if you claim
such realization,

get humble
and alone
for a time.
Learn to breathe.
Learn to read.
Learn to speak from the center.
Seek counsel from few
for few will understand.
But as you gain resonance
among the kindred, this will be
your way station in the
vast barrens
of love and suffering,
between long periods of
empty wandering that
most others will spurn by means of
religion or any movement
of the many. And be sure
to remember who you are
when watching a parade or
enduring a dinner party.
You will be
where you belong
soon enough,
among the poor,
free, with nothing to prove or

protect,
returning
again
and again
to the silence.

I Learned Upon Waking

I was dreaming,
in which a little Sherpa man
came to me and said
any of the world's great religions
is a means of unraveling
into the unity.
I was amused
he then used
a bar room idiom to
further his conjecture: *So,*
what's your poison?
With a smidge of dread
I asked "is any one better
than another?",
to which he said, in
foxhole vernacular,
smoke 'em if ya got 'em.
Just before I opened my eyes
I thought to ask,
"Who guides the Sherpa?"

Coyote

He came to guide
the ready and able
beyond their borders.
He said, I will tell you of
the way
though it will be
inglorious for now.
Through the many
deaths and births of life,
this is your lot as one
sentient of animal time
and consequence of spirit.
Remember
the sipapu in the
floor of the kiva.
Remember
the downward plunge
behind boulders in the river.
Remember
the first step out the door
on the journey of ashes.
These mark the way of passage.
But because
you have the olden knots in your head,
you will need to listen

to the timbre of a
hallowed heart.
There you will find
the substance
that ages your face with
initiation and portion, enough
for this endeavor though
best rendered cipher until
your words are bent in
wisdom and not in judgment.
See your core enwombed there as if
you are about to be born into the
hands of a new God,
for this is where He midwifes.
Listen well,
for is it not the trickster
who speaks in the
mother tongue of faith?

It Is Time

It is time you do
who you are.
It is time to
be one
with yourself and now.
It is a soft circle
you draw around
your own divisions.
It is a love
for all you thought left out.
It is the next step
while not knowing, it is the first
breath while still dying.
For you are gold of sun
cast once alone
into the human strain, and
only for a time.
You need not be prepared
but to the beauty
of being
broken open
to grace.
Even your sin trails off
as the spitfire incarnation
of some blazing glory.

You are your own
medium assigned to
gifts and wonders from
within to without
through which the light of a
vast mystery is refracted.
You bend it so sublime.

Portugal

This morning
I built a fire and
had a conversation with the sky
about bringing rain.
I wondered
if a particle of smoky ash could
ride the wind to Portugal,
touching down
in the sunlit hair
of a brown eyed girl.
She was taught to pray
to the mother of Jesus,
thinking in terms of
a heavenly kingdom, angels, saints
and channeled through crosses and cathedrals.
But she loves the seashore
where the world washes up
into her fledgling spirit
and the
shells in the sand
are her treasures.
Someday
she may
know.

Fernweh

Moonrise was waiting
on the turning earth
to send it on its modest arc
across the southeast corner
of the starry dome. I was out
to warm the car,
anxious to catch up with Boston,
two hours ahead into the day.
Jet planes are time machines. Yet,
the sky stood me still.
I lingered.
I noticed how often I stop
to look up,
watching, and wanting
to get back to something;
to be where I was
before
I became distracted
by satellites.

My House on Sachem Street

These forty years
have diminished your dimensions
or expanded mine, house,
when held alongside my memories.
Having walked around Walden Pond
this morning, this evening
I rest upon your porch
where once I sat
for a single photograph
on a day when I was happy, and my
mother smiled softly
at that image of her son.
Your patina, as apparent as mine, and
each speaks of our years apart and
all the days I hungered for your refuge.
But I am loved, house, and
the dreams and prayers that
diffused through your walls
have often returned
to live in places far away,
in other houses where
I spoke of you
and the porch on which I sat
on a day when I was pictured yours
and you, mine.

Satellite

I walk in
to wait in line for a
small coffee and a
seat by the window
to watch
as Massachusetts Avenue flows
into a red brick way station
where the future
is calculated
four years at a time.
Out on the sidewalk, a
German Shepherd puppy is
tethered to a light pole,
wincing and whining at the
surging of
buses and bikes,
cars and hurried feet.
I scribble in my notebook
and read a brief passage
from Huxley's epic.
It seems I come
to these things late
and out of place.
When the last of my coffee is cold
I walk out

and bend down to
scratch the ears
of the dog. She
nuzzles up into my hand for
a little more on the chin.
My world is a small one
outlying larger spheres.
I walk away,
enter my orbit and
leave for the long way home.

Vestige

I would have chosen
a higher level of consciousness
had I been informed of my options
at the time of my birth.
Not knowing,
there I lay
gurgling
beneath the tricky combination of
my mother's
joys and fears.
My father,
in transit
from boot camp to base,
sailed the sea with Elvis,
in the tricky combination of
involuntary service.
I was
six months old
and had waited
my whole life
to meet him;
subjects
of world powers,
the fiercest

of which
on high, and
beneath our skin,
propriety,
sat on wooden pews
in itchy clothes
and learned of God,
again,
a tricky combination.
What of
a higher consciousness?
What of a skill so human
as to set
a son, a brother, a father
against it all?
It is that
one
can learn
to read his culture,
remove it from his bosom,
hold it up to the light,
tear it down,
bend it with his mind.
For it is

in the decoding
of tricky combinations
that tyrants are sent packing
and little boys
are set free.

Glass Jar

After the divorce
and in the throes,
I walked along the beaches
of Southern California
sunset after sunset.
I collected stones
and shells that I have kept
in a hand blown glass jar
I found at a rummage sale,
green,
cylindrical,
with air bubble imperfections
as if to suggest
a frailty,
perhaps a looming likelihood of
breaking open at
some point,
though now,
twenty-five years on my shelf,
holding steady
to the end of something,
reminding me
of the beginning of everything.
A shell is one half of an older life.
A stone, a fragment of an older earth,

washed over smooth,
silent and waiting.
A glass jar,
like a memory of experience,
a mere form in which to hold
the artifacts of history,
once living, now
sacrament.

When Lost in the Order of Things

Ask the stars for wildness
and you will get it
in formless disorder.
Nature is the giver
of the needed adventures.
Take it in
to discover you are in it.
You had it backward
and inside out
all the while.
That is why
you were asking
to begin with.

Sandy Hook

Five million square miles of arctic tundra
lie northward of most people
living on our planet.
The ungulates dwell there, and bears,
with fish swimming below and
birds flying above, and
the surface of the deep blue sea
covers one hundred and thirty-nine million more
of those square miles
that are treacherous
by nature
yet far from humans.
Latitude by longitude, if
God
were to be found
on the grid
it would be
in the crosshairs, then gone
before us,
above and below us,
nailed between the heavens
and the earth
for every innocent
wasted by fear, or
madness,

taken in the day.

He will begin again.

I think there might be

flowers growing on the stars.

It would take seventy-five quadrillion earths

lined up in a row

to reach across our galaxy.

Tender

I look up
in this red morning
to see the mountains
shouldering their clouds.
I feel the Gulf of Mexico
in the air,
cool on my skin,
laced with a shiver
of old world spirit,
like a walk in the
French Quarter past
crypts built like little castles
for the bones of haunters.
Later, this afternoon,
I will drive my tractor
crisscross in Colorado.
I am lost in the particular these days,
I myself particulate,
a bit of dust
driven by the rains
into the earth
for amending this
forsaken soil,
for the tending
of tall grasses.

Mercy

I walked into the wild, the
high country, a silence,
the first to the end of
that sky canyon,
no sight of
human tracks before me
on the last of winter's
great snow embankments.
I was held
in my footsteps
along
fields of fallen rock,
above
hidden torrents.
When I arrived,
I realized it is
all and nothing for
one like me.
I left what I could
in the deep water, yet
still
lose myself
in dreams
that vie
within me.

The Wound

The day comes you learn
what will take you by death.
Not by what kills the body, but
something other
by way of
a wound
that will never heal.
It will be yours alone
first sensed through love,
one for the ages.
It is caused
by holding desire
that will never leave you or
having desire fulfilled ever so
briefly
and then not.
All in all
it is sacred,
the portal through which
you pass to the grace
of humility.
Bear this wound
until your last breath.
Speak little of it
because, for most,

it is beyond understanding.
In the living of this mystery,
the wound,
as real as earth
is borne
to tear your heart open
to the sky,
to let your spirit be it's
winged avatar.
You will never know why
the wound
beyond bearing
will be your bearing home.

II

Trailhead

On the mountain's
jagged edge,
notched for canyon passage,
beneath the clouds
there sets a space
open to the far horizon for
blue and light to chase
the drear back over my shoulder,
out across the plains.
This reminds me
to do at least two things; one,
to find within
old fears of all
once thought so right
and real and heavy,
and two, to
build a cairn of them
before I go.

Ecotone

Having withdrawn
from the contest,
I live on the edge of town
with a mind for mountains.
I learned that dogs will follow
if you point your feet
in the other direction.
As does
the heart
pounding whole
in places where
musk of warm earth
vapors with the fragrance of spruce.
There is always only one world.
It is simple yet
confounding
to walk the line
between
culture and nature.
One is where
transcendence is possible
for a few.
One is where
it is.

Sangre De Cristo

Your rains have poured through me
and the dust of your trails is golden
on the bedrock of my inward spaces.
Your substance is of the original dream,
the stuff I too am made of;
dust and water,
flesh and blood.
Body to pain,
mind to wonder,
spirit to invocation.
Lay me low,
hold me close,
until I hear
the silence fixed
in
crags and crevice.

Minong, The Good Place

There is an island
in Lake Superior
inhabited by wolves,
and as with all things
that lie northward
from wherever I am
it is calling me
through an ancient boundedness.
Once over the chop,
stepping off the float plane,
there would not be a moment's hesitation and
no one else's fears
would cause me to have my own.
In being restored
from contrivance,
some seven days hence
at trails end,
having listened to songs returning,
hung misty on morning waters,
ringing in the rocks,
held tender in boughs of spruce and birch,
I will have lived
an entire lifetime
in silence.

To Listen to Everything

He leaves the house before dawn,
stands under the moon
and that single morning star,
to listen;
a torrent within,
outside,
the northbound train,
the dogs in the hills serenading the end of night,
the interstate humming.
In the far cottonwood,
an owl
speaks of the first world.
The man feels neither pure nor holy
but carries an instinct
some greater sphere
that joins with him
is held in pure holiness.
He lifts an inward request up to first light,
to live well with longing as it lingers.
He senses counsel to
step into the demeanor
of moons and stars.
He feels the strength to live
with feelings he cannot resolve,
to follow love

where it leads

to a simpler life

of waiting

for all that he desires

to come to him

in its time

and

if it chooses,

to drain him of his furies.

Pueblo

He was lost
in Pueblo, Colorado,
on the street,
standing in hard wind
and brittle sunlight.
He was abject and worn and
was familiar with Becker's *The Denial of Death*. I asked:
"When did you occasion such a volume?"
He was nebulous and shifty
as a man with bad secrets.
His skin was gray,
his breath, a rancid pall of smoke and whiskey.
He mumbled a few more words
about a *causa sui*
that had stolen his longing for joy.
When I wakened, he hung ghostly
off my left shoulder until my stupor lifted.
As I looked out
the bathroom window,
over the creek lit in moon and luminous pollution, for
there is no darkness anymore,
I reasoned him some share of
my spiritual atmosphere,
a grizzled mass of unclaimed dearth.
I read that book when I was twenty-nine,

mending from my divorce,
wheedling on a return to seminary
and sensing that I was with no one
and was no one, homeless but for
the world before me,
the occupant of one life, living
in one place.

August

In first light,
the distant northbound
bellows of its empty coal cars.
I have heard prayers like that.
Lowly moans of dogs are
lilting across a field of dew.
The prodigal monsoons,
seven years astray,
returning,
swelling the creek,
catalyzing the garden,
a hope for harvest.
A prompting,
spoken clear,
"pay attention",
this is August,
the season of
waiting and hunger.

Walk Out

I filled the feeders
with a sense
of having lost
connection
with the birds.
I hope they will forgive.
The ground
I walk on
is asking
my feet to
remember.
It spoke upward
into me and said
presence
will not be rendered
in off-site locations
or in programs run by
so called professionals.
If mine is
a path
made by walking
then first I must
walk out
on many things

and wait
for the birds
to return.

Rascal Wind

If you are ready
to take up with
the unknown,
begin with what you know; something
you can see, or hear, or touch or taste or smell.
From there, by way of
natural allegory, the
dark matter
will move through you
and the wild
will rustle at
the edges.
As in this wind,
that can only be felt
like a rascal
who taps on your shoulder
from outside your line of sight, you may
understand little
of its origin and purpose,
but much of its effects:
the emptying of bird feeders,
the gathering of dull dust in doorways,
the snaring of a neighbor's errant grocery bag
twisting in your fence, that
twinge of irritability within.

It's fine to curse its wiles, but also,
you may want to sigh
with some wiser resignation
that this rascal wind,
in the earliest hints of Spring
is teaching you
of unknown things.

Invitation in Blue Dusk

I sensed
a rush of wings above, a
sudden river flowed
in skyward waves, a
twisting spiral
random convergence
leading itself
centerless,
to inspire
its own innovations
and my silence. First,
of the crunchy growl
of boots on hardening snow.
Then breath, held,
for the sake of listening.
Then, mind entrancing
in its parallel flight
with this murmuration,
a sacred moment
of knowing
how to be
in the world.

In the Dark

In the dark
of winter's night,
the trees release their
salvage into fair exchange
with the breathing.
This is an aged and wisened love.
Enter the season,
and much has fallen off and away,
subject to the effect of
natural circumstance,
a learned method of thriving,
braced against the cold.
Remaining rooted, still longing
but now for the purest
of what love is; naked of the
leaves of youth and
verdant passions,
referring the beloved
unto the stars,
in the darkest night
hung shining above the
trees deep breathing.

Those That Come and Go

There are those that stay
and those that come and go.
The sun rises either way, the
creek flows as it did
a thousand years ago.
Our little histories intermingled
within the way
of the world.
And the world is its own
and we can only belong to it.
Yes, our hearts break
and hard
when we lose the love
we think we need
to keep from floating off
into some fearsome oblivion.
We hold to all the tender memories
as if to oxygen itself
until we breathe
that which makes for more
the common and the steady, the
real and the ready. The
deeper joy is yet to be
as we fade and age into

the ones that stay, and
share with all the world
those that come and go.

Bound Away

Their rivers have surged too strong
for this familiar dale,
their currents coursing to
broader valleys and farther seas.
Being is an empty absolute, for now is
to do,
to task,
to venture outwardly on the
who
they will become. We send them
wrapped in prayers
with songlines from our brighter dreams.
We fly our flags unfurled and
keep our fears to burn in our own fires.
Though breaking hard on grief
we wait
as they ascend the mountain alone
to drink from ancient headwaters
and quest along the sacred, dangerous places.
God is asking much of us, so
we summon our faith
they learn to live alongside
the wolf we call this beautiful world.
Only then will they draw their sustenance

from the vernal spring that flows
of both the minerals and the spirits,
the earth and the sky.

Signs and Wonders

I conjured
a curiosity of
Sandhill Cranes, on
an October Saturday morning,
in the thousands and for hours,
in droves one after the other,
passing, pausing,
circling back as if
at some critical juncture
in their migration, lingering
just above my house.
I could feel at once
the arc from Nebraska to New Mexico
along the Platte River watershed, they,
breeding bound 'til death,
weaning chicks to winged freedom,
released upward within this
rattling constellation
slung across my sky.
Wintering here
then summering there,
born and gone in twenty years
having etched a line through
blues and grays in each.
For what I was witnessing

I thought there might be
some local coverage, or a
giddy gathering
of binoculared watchers,
a flourish of tweets, posts, pics, but
none that I could find.
Perhaps a poet, a photographer,
a painter,
a newspaper man,
a hazy old hippie or two,
not one. I wished to see, at least
a friend, arriving in haste,
not bothering to close the car door
but running
to the meadow,
to stand alongside,
to fall quiet
but for breathing,
enraptured,
to watch,
to listen, and
read the sign of the
Sandhill Crane.
But no one came.
I wondered.

Odd Goose

Mystery is the offside
of everything we see.
For what we each
have always been
is an embodied consciousness
somehow knowing and
not knowing all at once.
Feel free
to make sense of it all,
how you choose,
with words you gain
along the learning.
String them together and
weave them into your finer accessories
of contemplation. However,
be sure to make time for
breathing in
the substance of
actual experience
somewhere between the
conception and the writing.
Sometimes words are better followers.
Leave room

for something other,
for the occasional
odd goose.

The Old Fence

This morning
I shucked off the notion of routine
and took a walk in the cold.
The deer I had not seen in days
flushed out of the willow brush,
cantered along the frozen creek.
They knew the ice was
one night thin.
The old buck,
sensing that I might be
snagged in a broad wariness,
turned and kept his eye on me.
I noticed
the old fence I built years ago
with second-hand materials
needs to be taken up
from the ground
and hauled away.

Turning

Autumn is burning,
turning,
all green grown is suddenly fire,
lit from within in the fading dusk.
The vital hue descending,
to the root we all go,
to our essential darkness, but not before
our luminous colors reveal
the passing of our substance,
our earnest quest
for some small and holy godhood.
One last flare into the coming night!
One fierce instinct to speak love
into the span of all that is.

House of Time

On the north side of the house
the furrowed skin of the peachleaf willow
chafes into the gray,
gathering nourishment and
winter's camouflage, a proper
blind for a band of mourning dove,
cooing in chalky plumage,
lit by the dawn's diffusion.
Across the creek,
the Redwing Blackbirds buzz aloft
in the bare cottonwoods
to devise their being
in the element of now.
It is a cruel human aptitude
to see around corners
or too far into the future, and
to set one's pace by chimes
or alarms, or calendars.
Counting days is a miserable tyrant.
I begin too many
determined to live backward
from the moment of my death to today,
a strategy taught to me by Thanatos himself.
Though by now, I have lived in this house
more days than any other house,

for a decade of days,
this house on the creek flowing
with the blood
of willows and cottonwoods,
has coursed into me
from the earth.
I am held here
against the perennial foreground.
I walk out
into eternity every morning.
This is the place my children leave me
standing, rooted, refuged, time and again.
This is the place to which a
broken heart will haven from a rite
that leaves the other in the wind,
the surest passage
into the now of Blackbirds.

The Coldest Day of the Year

I

Sit close to the fire, friend.
We will pour the coffee
and warm our hands.
The plow is on the truck,
the tractor is in the barn.
The dogs that would otherwise
snort off the call indoors are
curled and closing their eyes.
Now, we wait for the snow to fall
from the seams
between the morning stars.
Let's sit and talk
of our memories
of years as children
of the North.
The wind might tell us
of its purpose.

II

We have no need
to hold the coming storm
in an unwise contempt.

We hardly understand ourselves,
so, let alone the weather.
We live on a mountainside
raised by the quaking earth
and polished by glaciers.
The genetic code that
shapes our bodies and our being
has been found in bones that are
four hundred thousand years old.
We are just the current stratification.
Our vigor for health and increase is
equal to the forces wrought of a
beautiful world.
These are of the unity,
the light
and the virtues.

III

The trees are lit
for tis the season
and though my Christ

has long transfigured cosmic,
I see within you
the nature of that fabled infant.
It seeps out from under all
you have learned to believe, all
you have swallowed
through your ears;
The cacophony of misconstructions
about the double-mind,
the falsehoods
and the turpitudes.
We will no longer listen
to those who yearn for heaven
while stuffing their own stockings
full of coal.
Our life is not a game
of penitence, but
of becoming
who we already are.
I too concur
and now infer
the truth of advent
that kindles the flame of our spirits
on this, the coldest day of the year;
like the child we herald
come to band with our faith,
you, my brother, and

you, my sister, are
whole,
you are true, and
you are good.

Samuel

The wind
of early Spring is a
hard-bitten woman.
She draws me dry
of idyllic bliss,
makes me work the harder
to stand straight up
in this world.
There is no care in her bluster
and though she is cold and capricious,
I lean into her harsh graces
and divide her
as with a wood wedge
melded of earthen mineral,
wrought from spit and fire.
I curse my trials until I am conscious.
Then, I see the love
in what I would not readily choose.
This night I am Samuel,
and I hear that voice calling,
thinking of it
as my madness
when all along
the stars are resonating
with the original dream

carried to me
on the bitter winds
of early Spring.
Speak Lord, your
servant is
listening.

On a Cold Morning
After the Spring Storm

With mountains
sheathed in crystalline mist, while
all is cloaked in white and still,
as Winter lingers
into the new season,
for what it would give
to the ground, there is
only the wait
and the breathing,
the fire and the
warm cascade of
coffee merging
with a tempered surrender,
a learned easiness
into which the day unfolds.

Chasm

To be removed from office,
your station in life, your cubicle of
institutional distinction. To play host
to an occupational meltdown, an imposed or
self-induced professional annihilation.
To watch your vocational membrane, the one
that made you feel viable and decent,
molt into the wind of disregard, of no account, of
yesterday. As if you woke from a fall at the
bottom of a broken ladder, to feel the bleak
void of mid-morning on weekdays, of
mid-life, of mid-meaning, unsure where to
place sporadic poise while
nagging anguish throbs between sessions of
self-interrogation; Remember, as you may
have been mistreated, by others or yourself,
speak little of it. A bitter heart needs time to
foment in blessed seclusion, away from ears
unworthy of your tangential complaints.
You might avoid that murky puddle of primal fear
and get careful with all that enters
your mental panorama.
You are going to need some strength.
Be as quiet as you can.
Breathe deeply and while you let your eyes turn

upward in your swirling skull

from one moment to the next,

pause, rest, cease.

This is your task for a time;

pause, rest, cease, until you perceive

a great chasm dropping off

before your feet

and hear

these

words:

you

will

reach

the

other

side

though

not knowing how or when.

For now, you have distances

to consider. You are taking on

a new sense of precious time.

You have the dangers

of a rightful modesty to navigate

for you have been tried and convicted

of being human. You have the crucible

of vulnerability to endure

as the dross of your inward nonessentials

surface above the fire of
asking the Universe for temperance,
for a steely purpose,
for a place of belonging.
And as it may not be obvious
that you will find a wider plain
on which to trade
in the market of fairer commerce,
you will.
On the turning point
from playing a dumb role to
working from the center of your soul,
the reason for descent comes clear:
you had chasm work to do
for which
our world
will be
rewarded.

Canyon

If there is a virtue
like water, something
real, working down,
to darkness unknown,
to depths only sensed,
never seen;
then become
this canyon
willing to give up
on stately profiles
standing sheer on far horizons.
Channel a quenching
from those whitened peaks.
Carry life to dry places.

Spacious

Coyote are wise
and know how to be
in the world. When one dies
another moves in
and takes the place.
They keep good sense
of spatial relations
while humans do not.
Out on the edge, in California,
there is not enough to go around
and the greater bounding box falls off
into a violated ocean.
The people must watch each other
too carefully
and I wonder
how their poets
are faring.
Meanwhile, back home,
our local experts
decided to move
seven coyote
to "wilder" territory,
but I do not know why.

Soon I saw seven more,
spread out nicely
where seven coyote belong,
being who they are.

Poem, Untitled

To live
beneath the tongue
before tasting of the things
I make meaning of.
Instead,
to sense the ground below my feet,
the north wind on my neck, the
winter death of grass,
the piercing light of stars, the
weight of moving water,
the huffing breath of dogs,
the woman's touch on skin, and
how the night
cradles everything in close
to soothe the ways of words
to sleep.

Let Us Throw Our Ideas into the Fire

Take any idea
that we herald as gospel
and ask at which point
along history's timeline
was it invented,
by whom,
and for whom,
and then ask
at which point did
the supposition become
irreproachable dogma?
Then,
what effect did this tenet
have on the people for whom
it became so unimpeachable?
Finally, as of today,
we should ask
is this old idea
lost to its
first-born meaning?
Then watch as time passes as
those who pose challenge
are vilified asking

for reasons and options.
They have burned at the stake,
they have died in the dungeon,
today, they are cast off
to live in the margins.
For certain the danger
is that of a concept
that cannot be challenged
or thrown in the fire,
for fire would only
make that worth the keeping
more pure and far truer
than any unquestioned.

If You Will Have Me

I hope to die
into my life,
surrender to
its pain and pleasures,
moving easy, like
mist on water, a
leaf in wind, and
not speak of it
beyond a subtle nod
to the universe.
Having struggled
with dispossession
for so long,
then, by my stars,
I reached a pitch of absurdity
as if listing
into a great fall
from pretense.
It is good to fail
brilliant and slow
and send it all
flaming far into horizons.
This is the light of the world.
If this world will have me in my

state of grace, I will
stay on,
keep breathing
until I learn
to love.

Leaving for Home

When we wake,
stand and walk
from the world
we were raised in,
life becomes itself.

III

Legacy

The poet knows
a terrible joy of writing
into dust and breath
a gathering substance,
a formed oneness
that stands itself up
to walk away into
this beautiful world,
whole and on its own,
never to return
to the cerebral gunge.
For this beautiful world
demands all
and will take all.
And what it takes
it will return
in words.
In the ashes
and the wind,
we will only have
the words.

Far Side of a Lonesome Star

I was a sophomore in college,
sober, though not clear-minded,
and certainly, a common discontent.
I was searching.
I was sitting
in a chair
in a room
with a friend.
We were talking
about a poem
I had written
of the movement
of the earth
on its axis,
more precisely,
how it first was nudged
into turning
as it does
once it came to rest
in its orbit.
Suddenly I, or some part of
my sense of things
was suspended in space
on the far side
of a lonesome star

lit by an unseen source,
distant and unknown.
I was safe, warm and fearless.
However, more thunderously
silent and piercing
was the presence
I felt.
This is the first I have spoken of it.
Let me say,
for the sake
of owning my experience,
I think I may have seen
everything at once, or
perhaps everything
I ever needed to see.

Seed

This is the
natural progression of things:
the seed grows
in the husk
then the husk sloughs off.
Know the difference. There is
no arrogance in either. If
you must make something
of a shell you no longer need,
do it with love.
But when you feel the wind
slant and soft
on the break of some new morning,
all you have to do is
fall.
Be the seed
you are, germinating in this soil
of present life.
Be,
open to everything,
Stay here, go deep.

A Darker God

I have come to know
of a darker God.
There are hours in the night
when He is formless and void,
beyond all that is.
Impersonal and elsewhere,
He is the frightening spaciousness
that swallows the universe whole.
He is
in stark contrast
to all claims and constructs.
The moment He is imagined,
He is not imagined.
The moment He is described,
He is not described.
He is of no gender
beyond awkward human language.
He is utterly unaware of religion
and bears no impulse toward
the chanting of creeds or the
wrenching of pleas.
He is from nowhere
and headed toward nothing.
He is boundless,
vast

and unspeakable,
never to be found.
I did not love God
until I learned of a darker God, and
surely, He leads me out beyond
all reaches
of human desperation and endeavor.
When I begin in the dark,
I am free.
When I begin in the dark,
finally,
I know how to pray.

New Rain

In faces of the young
or those inspirited likewise
I see
a great turning
toward one;
a singularity
of creation and its
source. Without much
in the way of
agency, but for the
divine rites of science
and poetry,
human consciousness
is being drawn out in the
zeitgeist,
vaporized of its
harder elements and
taken up
by the sun
for the making
of a new rain,
for the sake of
a nurturing sustenance
of earth, our only home.
This is the faith

revealed in the
nuance of all faiths.
Each one of us, or that
to which we hold is
a drop
once of the original firmament
and thus burning off,
rising, returning.
We learn of this faith in our
vast array of better stories, tales
contrived by necessity.
We move with this faith as
it dissipates into silent mystery.
We become this faith
when we finally
fall like rain
as love.

Morning by Morning

In the smoke of many fires
we rise.
Our signals are read
across the far reaches.
Morning by morning,
taken up,
taken in,
braiding skyward
into the wild dream
yet spilling out with star fall
flaring
silent
four billion years,
resting here,
cooling, revolving, wettening,
conceiving, generating, incubating,
cultivating, nurturing, caring,
loving
its own
by its own nature.
Its consciousness, we,
waking,
watching,
returning as the dream itself,
becoming it,

rising,

morning by morning,

in the smoke of many fires.

Dreamed

It can be a long pause
between breaths
when one is dwelling on
the source of things, or in
learning
the red
caught in the cloud net
at dawn
comes from elsewhere,
never ours to fully understand.
We make mystery a
fun house mirror image
when we claim to know.
Take your breath
as any creature would.
I think we are free here.
It is I, you, we and
all the world
being understood,
beheld,
dreamed.

Redwing

Red Winged Blackbird sang
of the expanse of all things,
of the sacred emptiness of plain spaces.
I walked beneath
his melodic teaching three mornings
as if I needed to hear it again
and once more.
The dogs appeared
to have the lesson well in hand
though I struggled
to hold it long enough
to bring it to heart.
I still have many suspicions
so, Blackbird sent me
around and rapt on the trail
as he loosed into a northerly squall.

This Day

This day is for
breathing in and
breathing out.
This day is for walking
long and quiet
on the trail
by which the waters flow.
This day is for the
ever changing landscape of
the heart conjoined in
all that is.
I fell through the floor of my religion, out
into the sunlight of
present silence.

A Hollowed Place

When my spirit
is weary
of bearing my burdens,
I fade off trail
to a hollowed place
of unknowing,
and let everything fall.
I slip into a healing sleep,
to waken
sometime later,
during the last lingering moment
of one of God's dreams, and
wrapped in a Hudson Bay blanket.

Sail

For a time, we harbor.
We live among our own, in
bounds of law
and whims of culture.
There are mores
and norms
and rituals
to observe,
for we believe
that God inhabits them.
In the teaching of children
lies the distillation of our substance.
A learned scrutiny
will reveal our absolutes. Yet,
there is a means of measured anarchy
in the heart of the awakened.
We church ourselves along
until we are called away
to sail the curve of the blue earth
broiling in the first sun.
We only spoke of horizons then.
Now,
in quite small numbers
and out through the narrow channel,
we are navigating
around a new world.

Kingdom Come

And the angel
said to Mary,
There is a world
within the world
that is the world
that will be.
Once it is held dearly
without care for
its origin, it has
no other way but
to be born to
the one real world.
You will be
within
what is
within you.
This is the kingdom come.
This is the way of
all dreams.

Incarnatio

Be born
you
into the ineffable
and empty consciousness
within all things,
revealed in the deeper evolutions,
streaming from nothing to nowhere as
one silence to one silence, as
enfleshment through woman's womb, as
broken bread through suffering,
through pain and darkened portal, as
one love to one love when
all is finally hung upon the tree.
So, become such giftedness
to grace this night,
to veil the moon in mystery,
and now,
to light this day
as sun to soul,
each one of us,
be born.

Advent for a Wolf-Child

I am a shepherd
waiting on stars,
brooding
for this age
on a bright one.
Each generation must resolve you see,
we must, again,
make our way through this mystery.
The same old greatest story ever told
is swept under the wonder again.
I can see you
hiding,
alone,
beneath this brilliant nightscape.
You claim the legend for your own
though your substance wanes
within your customs.
If unknowing is not your thing,
you can, let us say, for a moment,
go savage,
through instinct,
become a child raised by wolves.
Come stunned, undone,
feel it all for the first time
without the words you are inflicted with.

Come out
into the darkness
from that cleft in the rock
you call your life.
Shudder beneath the
lightning voices
igniting a million miles of
nerve cells flashing
from your reptilian stem
to the toes of your heedful feet.
Wolf-child!
Lift your chin!
Breathe deep the funk of
mammalian birth,
the musky blood and tears,
the steaming hide of oxen, donkey dung
and the dog in sympatico panting.
Come alongside mother
bathed in fevered mirth in this
earthen enclave womb of light.
Now, wolf-child, rejoice;
you have seen this hiddenness,
one come native,
who joins with all of human faith,
the revelation of the

original dream
unfolding still,
a sense of who we are.

Keystone

To be free
from the darker arts,
the contriving of forms reversely onto the
foreground of natural history.
Soothsayers gazing backwards,
trading the naked now for
trinkets of lore and laud,
we trouble ourselves with tradition,
we glory in our conquests
of the lesser then.
If Jesus was anything
more than a man, he was a wolf.
Seething into our herd of ailments,
his iridescent eyes grew fixed
in a chilling stare at the
ensuing death
of the first great human distortion:
dominionism.
No wonder we killed him as we
kill him today. We dress him in purple
and crown him with
jagged misattributions. He was
predator come to thin the
ranks of our diseased confidences,
to strengthen our substance

within a remnant.
As with any whose truth
is too real to destroy,
he haunts our dreams
and howls to the moons of our
deepest instincts.
He has done his bloody work
and left
those of us still standing
to walk
each trail of faith that leads
to the new earth.
Let us see
creation as it is.

Sabbath

I remember
what I knew of Sabbath
before I learned
a broader way to be it,
now held
with the understanding
of things so wide
as to make me small, and
for the taking up of
being
right where I belong.
I walk happy
on the perennial journey
from form to faith.
You see, when Sabbath rises
into each day,
the dew ferments
on fresh cut grass
so my nose and lungs
ride tandem in
musky camaraderie. That too,
my head, my heart, my hands
are joined in praise.

I say, *this is everything*, learning
to rest.
I have come to
observe it.

On Whom to Invite to the Feast

Come to be,
out of words.
Come to be in need of something holy,
something you cannot find
where you most often clamor.
Come alone to the wild place
resigned and fallow to stand
where the contours of earth are traced
by wind and light.
Come to the fire of hunger
casting the fury of your own shadow.
Prepare the meal in silence.
There is a work being done, unknowing,
a wedding in Cana in need of its company.
Beyond the usual and ordained,
invite
the orphan of hiddenness,
the quiet, unfulfilled desire.
Invite a tempered anonymity.
Invite the contradiction and contrary.
Invite the prodigal and his brother.
Invite fear and reluctance.
Invite the deed done unheralded and
the deed performed in shallow pride.

Invite the squandered moment.
Invite ignorance and her twin sister certitude.
Invite envy and smallness, arrogance
and the loose regret. Invite the
denied. Invite the dispossessed.
Invite the stranger within
whom no one has known
or loved. Invite the exile.
Invite the infidel, and yes,
invite the trickster,
to whom you owe a
great debt.
When the proclamation of the feast
has echoed far and wide,
and all seems ready,
wait now, and watch;
for from the vast horizons
will come the often unwelcomed guests of
actual character,
legion within a kaleidoscope soul.
Place a ring on fingers, a robe on shoulders.
Watch each disfigured face alight in
awed relief, blossoming the deeper beauties out
into the music and the laughter.
Let the raucous celebration resound
into the night,
for this is the great homecoming.

And there, at the threshold
glowing sure against the darkness,
besmirked and coy,
arriving almost too late:
the words.

Sunday Go to Meeting

No one asked
but if they did,
how should we build the church?
I would reply;
with the pews facing out
and the pulpit in the back, no
windows allowed,
all open air
even in winter,
and the altar
would be a long walk
into the forest, so
when one might rise
from kneeling
there would only be the
bright wind
stirring branches
lit in morning.

Everything Belongs

O, for faith beneath all faiths.
Each of us will live a
chosen way and
die somewhere
in the descent of it.
We, the unbound into consciousness
know that we are here,
resonant inward,
shining outward,
some notion of substance,
some foreknowledge of destiny.
Sooner, should we feel that
everything belongs
and ours is not to
pick and choose the matter
of all that is
but to love it whole again;
to repent
of being the product of contraptions,
religious and otherwise,
to flourish in the rooting
close to home and heart, from
dawn to dawn,
moon to moon,
blood to blood,

garden to garden, all
as one
to share.

Poems and Rivers

I am
of poems and rivers.
I stand
as it all
works around
my footing.
I am held,
wordless
and watchful.
While I fish,
while I write,
waiting on delight,
a fight,
not knowing
what's next,
a broad turn
downstream,
a desperate run
to hidden structures,
a sudden gasp at
twisting flight then
plunging to
dark freedom.

I am
of poems and rivers,
immersed,
worked upon,
smoothed, and
someday
carried off,
to be found.

Emerger

Beneath the stone,
encased in stillness, dark and cool,
larvae strains to pupae strains
to nymph, then bubbled for transport
rising, emerging, surfacing,
enticing Browns and Rainbows suspended.
Resting, waiting upon the flow then
spreading anxious into first
flutter, an embodied gasping for
first exchange, struggling
into the thinner, dryer, warmer medium,
fluttering, lifting,
falling,
fluttering, lifting
falling,
fluttering, lifting… flying
in spinning allurement of those below, and now
still rising
against the yellow sky,
belonging to it and everything,
the wind now leading
to the green love of willow brush
and resting again,
set above,
alongside
the depths once known.

Voyageur

He is of the North, and
prays in the way of
water and fire, elements of
journey, paddling through
an expanse of vanquish,
ravaged by love unrequited,
on voyage many years,
passage and portage, the
depths on one side,
the forest on the other,
a darkening mystery
below and above. Each
offer their bounty to the
North man for body and spirit
to subsume in creaturely endurance
and in the broader narrative; bestowments
of the wild God. He lies alone, fireside,
out under the stars
and near to his thoughts
on the suffering of the world,
his loneliness, and the
common yearning found in all
creation for some sense of
consummation that is always yet ahead,
not fully known, the great hunger

shared by all in striving forward
for survival or significance. No one
rests but for the dead.
He dreams of returning
home, taking his woman into his
arms, drawing her alongside his
desires by the small of her strong
back, waiting for her to sense
her yes to him, her wanting him
as much. For now, he might
be more starbound than within her, for
he has been lost to himself for so long.
In the dawn, he eats his fish and
wild mushrooms, blueberries
on his oats, chased down by black coffee.
He reads his Jeffers as clear as a man
ever could and aches for the
despair of it. In setting off
with the new day,
in faith that knows
nothing, he has the water and
the fire, and for now
he can only be sure
he is being led.

The Veil

I leaned against the tailgate,
pulling on my waders,
rigging up my fly rod
after driving through mountains
to fish wider waters
in open country.
Out across the field,
sweeping away from the lake
there knelt an old antelope,
his folded legs beneath him.
He was still,
bent low, perhaps
to smell the sage
as medicine or
to wait for all the world
to leave his mind.
As I walked to the shore,
I thought of his life
being long and sometimes hard,
of his loves,
those here and those gone, and
of all he might have fathered
onto this vast plain.
I thought of how he wintered in the open,
through the darker nights, in the deeper snows.

For a moment, I wondered
if this were his time,
like an old Lakota
who might lie down
under a tree
and close his eyes.
I thought of how all the living things of earth
surrender,
though not easily the conscious.
The antelope was not finished
for when I returned
I noticed
he had walked off,
or perhaps just diffused
through the veil
that tosses
in my most restless dreams.

Upon the Death of a Friend

For Ansel

There is a certain lilt
in the whole of things,
so demure
yet so threatening to
the letter and the law
it must subtle itself in life forms
and experiences
that take hold in the
unguarded spaces of the heart.
The lesson is to learn to see
what one did not see coming,
to hear what speaks in gaps
of silence.
It is in the sway of the pine bough and
in the breath of the crow's wings.
It is in the marimba tone of the cowbird's throat
and in the jasmine's essence.
It is in the curtain of virga
and the nuzzle of a cool nose.
It is in the bitter swell
of the chest when walking
without the dog one loved.

It is in the teardrop.
It is in what was meant to be and then not.
It is in the chance
that our existence is small
while nothing and everything
teeters on it
after all.

Janus

The morning
will break.
This turning to that.
To view the edge
of the new
from the far side
of the old.
To be through
with what is meant
to go beyond.
To share the receding night
with light
and open
what was felt withheld
as a gift of other
and elsewhere
to a new day.

Light

I face the dawn
and all is silhouette
and shadow.
I turn away,
and all is lit
with a
soft awakening
that says, look!

About the Author

Over the course of his life, James Scott Smith has lived in Michigan, Massachusetts, Kansas, California and for the last 24 years, Colorado. He studied psychology and religion while beginning his work as a psychotherapist, a wilderness guide, and a spiritual leader. He went on to create and lead a system of learning organizations designed to deliver holistic, experiential intervention in traditional and alternative settings. Breaking from his formal career in 2006, James enjoys his children and home life, the Colorado backcountry, his dogs, photography and writing.

HOMEBOUND PUBLICATIONS

An Award-winning Independent Publisher Since 2011

Homebound Publications is a small press with big ideas.
As an independent publisher, we strive to ensure, that the mainstream
is not the only stream. It is our intention at Homebound Publications
to preserve contemplative storytelling. We publish full-length introspective works
of creative non-fiction, travel writing, poetry, and novels.
In all our titles, our intention is to introduce new perspectives
that directly aid humankind in the trials we face at present as a global village.

WWW.HOMEBOUNDPUBLICATIONS.COM

CPSIA information can be obtained
at www.ICGtesting.com
Printed in the USA
LVHW02s0036241017
553515LV00003B/3/P